unreciprocated

Unreciprocated

ISBN 978-0-646-81381-3

Illustrations by Annalise Batista from Pixabay.
Graphic design by Yokelin.

to the one who has changed me

about the writer

yokelin has never imagined that one day she would write poems
she rarely read books when she was little
but she developed a love for poetry as she grew older

yokelin turned to writing as a form of documenting her journey of
finding love, experiencing heartbreak and healing
her first poem was written in despair and feeling isolated

yokelin's writing is a collective emotions and feelings that
she has buried inside of her, too afraid to share openly
and fearing judgement from those close to her

through expressing her emotions in poetry
she starts to accept her emotions and began healing

contents

the book

i love this book
i met this book by fate and have fallen for this book by accident
i fell in love with this book right after introduction

this book is filled with warmth and vibrancy
every time i read this book, my heart is overwhelmed with joy
butterflies in the stomach, eyes glowing with affection
and my body involuntarily uplifts beyond its limit

i had plans to own this book, making it exclusively mine
but mid way through first chapter
i realised this book isn't meant for me
someone else has put this book on hold

my plan to be this book's owner crumpled overnight
my instinct told me to keep this book out of sight
and let my longing subside

but fate is playful with me, placing this book never too far but seldom near
this book sometimes calls for me but mostly stays distant

this book showers me with burst of attention
as though it could sense my lingering eyes
like the passing storms, it comes and goes with little weather warning
i sometimes dressed for the storms
but often inappropriately clothed for the weather

i caught a glimpse of confusion after a recent storm
as if this book longs for a different owner
someone who would love it the right way

i used to keep an open mind that one day this book would look for me
an owner who is never far so that i could love it the right way
but this book changes its colour too often
and too often rejects my hand reaching out to it

as time passes, thorns started to grow on its cover
it's too painful for me to hold on
i decided burning this book to ashes
is the only way to let go

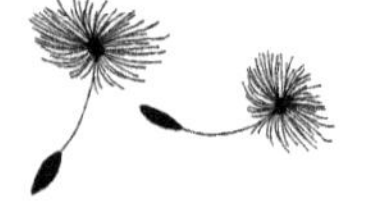

hope is lost

i am feeling down today
realising the hope i had is drifted away

i looked into the mirror
wondered many times why no one would love this face
i looked into my eyes
so much sorrow and tomorrow it goes away

i wanted to believe you liked me a little
i wanted to mingle
i wanted to forget you

i looked above and wondered why this test
realised it was to accept
what's not mine
what's not there
what's never meant

today i didn't cry
inside i whined
i'm not lonely but my heart is alone
i'm not dependent but i need reassurance
i'm not clingy but i wanted to stop longing
for the one who may never come

****thinking of you****

i think of you
at the first beat of a song
at the tone of amy's voice
at a picture of a black-eyed bear
at a look of a hand
at an outline of a silhouette
at a thought of a book

you are a book i liked at first sight
at the end of introduction
a book that i could never turn the pages
as the leaves were glued together
the strangers in the elevator
where i first met the barrier

i patiently waited
i carefully treated
i lovingly gifted
i attentively peeled back its pages
my heart broke
at the time i placed the book down
at the first step i took in walking away

i see you

i used to be eager to see your face the next day
now i wish i didn't have to see you on any day
coz for every time i see your face, i feel my heart break
every time i feel my heart plagued with pain

when we first met

i liked you the first time i laid my eyes on you
something about you made me feel warm inside
it could be your smile
or just the way your eyes dance when you smile
it was lovely to meet you

meeting room

i have forgotten when was the last time your eyes met mine
too long has passed as i gazed across the room
and so used to emotionally withdrawn
i neglected to engage my facial muscles
to greet you with a smile
i secretly wish i could turn back time and show you
what was on my mind as i looked into your eyes

the initiation

the less you want to initiate a conversation with me
the more i feel like i'm a pest
you said i don't bother you
but how you make me feel bothers me

unmeeting

is it possible to unmeet someone?
is it possible to remove memories of this one?
is it possible to forgive what's done?
is it possible to accept you're not the one?

scent of you

a squeeze of the nozzle
the scent rushing through
the fragrance it produced was something so allured
imagery of you appearing in my mind
forcing it to leave will take quite some time

the smell of you so attractive and benign
the thought of you so tender and kind
try guessing the brand became a game of mine
tick, tock, tick, tock
i lost track of time

missing you

i see you daily
i still miss you dearly
you are so close yet impossible to reach
your mind is always elsewhere
i don't even get a second
it hurts to see you smile at me
knowing you're just being friendly
i can't stop loving you
for you're the one i want to stay connected to

open mind

i keep an open mind that one day you would reach out to me
as days go by i think it's becoming more and more unlikely
so i become more and more available for you
more and more emotionally investing unconsciously
i need to pull myself out before i lose my sense of self entirely

you looked at me with such gentleness
knowing that you have hurt me
but your tenderness contains hesitation
reluctant to make it right for me
deep down i really believe
believing that you have noticed you care about me
just that it wasn't strong enough to do what's good for me

despise

i noticed you don't seek out my company
i concluded it is because you despise me

nursing heart

i was nursing a broken heart when you came into my life
the light i saw in your eyes became my loving guide
you're so beautiful, charming and kind
i lost the ache in my chest with you nearby

though the sweetness was short lived
your tenderness still has a hold on me
i want to forget you, forget you can read my mind
as though you were my soul mate but never will be mine
you're the worst kind of heartache
i wished i cannot feel it all the time

the light i once followed i wanted to dim with time
i resent the way you make me feel
how you came into my life
the reason you leave me behind

rejection

i invited you to connect
you replied with your silence
turning my heart to stone
it feels so cold when i see you
so ignorantly smiling at me
unknowing that you have hurt me
silence can kill
my feelings is your latest victim

sudden departure

i remember the first time i ended up next to you
your arm and mine touched
we both didn't move away
inside i smiled

i remember the last time i ended up next to you
your smile and mine greeted
you left swiftly without warning
headed to a corner of the room that felt safer than standing by me

the pain i felt was sipping through my smile
i mirrored your sudden departure
exited the fire pit that was burning my heart
i resented you for not noticing my broken

sweetheart

did you notice the connection between us?
it could fool others into believing that it's chemistry
the electricity in the air when our eyes meet is unstoppable

i deliberately hide the smile on my face
when you uncannily pluck words from my mind and made them yours

i held onto a block of sweetness i got for you
as i watched you received blossoms from your sweetheart

i regret for waiting too long
letting someone else stole the surprise i had planned for you

i'm thankful for having waited
it was a heavenly reminder that your sweetheart is not me

questions

i noticed the lack of details in your answers
that was when i stopped asking questions
what, why, when and how became irrelevant
your reluctance to reveal your true self was all i could focus on
our conversations dried out by the fear in your eyes
and awkwardness in your voice
your fear of rejection drowned your chances of
sharing a beautiful connection with anyone trying to get close to you
i gave up
on you

meeting you

i met someone who could read my mind for the first time
it was magical
sweet like chocolates
until i noticed the ring
everything changed
it became torments when words were stolen from inside my head
i became afraid of being close by
fight or flight
i chose latter

deep well

i give you all of my attention unconditionally
when i don't get anything in return it feels like i have fallen
into a deep well
crawling my way back up alone in the dark is exhausting
and i repeatedly make the same mistake for you

everyday

everyday i wait for you
everyday i get disappointed

everyday i see you
everyday i miss you

everyday i think of you
everyday i am forgotten

everyday i fall deeper for you
everyday i watch you fall deeper for someone else

brave & dumb

i was brave (and dumb)
i deleted your number
i won't be able to annoy you anymore
i want to continue to care about you (and i really do care so much)
but i don't get anything in return for caring about you
that makes me sad
i want to be happy
so you gotta go
i need to make room for happiness
you got my number
you can start caring if you want to be part of my happiness

stumble & free

i fell off
you were in touch
my heart was calm
it no longer races for you
it beats calmly for me
my head was filled with indecisions
not for the fear of rejection
but for the fear of hurting you
i paused on my response
i decided not to hurt you
the way you have hurt me
i am bigger
i am free
i feel fine

woman of my dream

you are the woman of my dream
i wish i could turn back time and tell you this when we met
then maybe i could have a chance to show you what you mean to me
you belong to someone else now
i have let go but it doesn't mean it changes this fact
you are still the woman of my dream
there is someone out there who is just like you
i believe it
i have to
believe it

independence

the saddest reality is i'm not on anyone's minds
because i've mastered the art of moving on

conflicted

i fear you when i see you
i miss you when i can't see you

i freeze when i hear your voice
i miss hearing you call my name

i shut you out when you speak
i get tongue-tied when i speak to you

i long for getting to know you
i stop myself from questioning you

feels

a few weeks ago
i let go of some feels
i feel lighter and my moods are brighter
the energy i get from knowing i will be okay
is enough to keep me up at night
i don't hear your voice as loudly as before
even though you're only a few feet away
the feels i let go have made room for different kind of feels
i like the new feels
i will keep these feels

this time of the year

this time of last year was the sweetest
this time of last year you reached out
this time of last year you were a follower
this time of last year you and i cheered
this time of last year you and i reconnected

this time of this year is the hardest
this time of this year i still miss you whom i can't have
this time of this year i still hear you whom i can't forget
this time of this year i still see you whom i can't speak to
this time of this year i still lie awake because of you

fake tan

you are as fake as the tan on you
the thing about fake tan is that
it fades with time
you will fade into the background
and become a distant memory

i used to see your beautiful face
all i see now is the unattractive fake tan
you labelled me "the inadequate"
i am enough for anybody
you are just not for me

i want to tell all your fans about your tan
how it needs to be reapplied in order to make you beautiful to the world
how this tan could never be applied on the inside and on your soul

you will forever be just that
a fake tan

empty promises

i heard it all before
you said you would keep in touch
days, weeks and months go by
not a genuine line you write

business is the only reason you call
"how are you?" is just an auto response
i said "you would never notice i'm gone"
that's a genuine line i write

kryptonite

you are my kryptonite
crippling my confidence when you're near by

you are my kryptonite
at a thought of you makes me tongue-tied

you are my kryptonite
holding my heart at ransom with all your might

you are my kryptonite
we need to be apart as we are worlds apart

nine to five

i exist between nine to five and five days
i am a ghost outside of the perimeter you set
guarding so attentively
i could feel your shield even when i'm asleep

silence

"be careful" she whispered
"i will"
there, tongue-tied
a moment she realised she cares for me
there, silence
a side of me she hadn't felt before
i care for you too

our story

i told her my story
she told me her story
the stories we told share similarities
we decide to write our story together
inspired by our vulnerabilities

mix tape

every time i miss you
i play our mix tape
i find myself playing the mix tape on repeat

alive

when i was talking to you
i feel alive
now you have left forever
i know what i needed in my life

who would have thought
conversations made of symbols and letters
could bring so much joy
then i realised, it was the feeling of being alive
that have kept me up at night

a connection with another soulful mind
feels like ecstasy in my veins
when you left without saying bye
i know i won't see you again

deep soul

has anyone told you that you have a beautiful face
your soulful eyes are where deep and dark secrets hide
your smile tells me that you have made friends with pain
that's why i like you more each day

three years on

remembering our cheers
reminiscing the clinks
ruminating the what ifs
recollecting our pain

confusing

the most confusing thing about our relationships with people
is we are connected 24/7 on social media
but we can feel disconnected at the same time

no to goodbye

i don't hang around on your way out
because being unavailable for you to say bye to
is the only thing i have control over whatever is between us

the vows

you etched my name on your heart
you hold my tenderness in your arms

i rest my love on your shoulders
i keep your secrets safe and sound

today we etched our vows on paper
from here on our love is etched on our souls forever

the abyss

i was a lifesaver buoy to you
you have found shore
i'm no longer useful
instead of taking me with you
you left me at sea, drifting alone
disappearing to the abyss of the horizon
it's so cold out there
but your heart is colder

connection

i'm always thinking of you
i'm too afraid to let you go
the only thing still connects me to you
is the thought of you

swift

i was beginning to enjoy being let in
but you closed the door to your heart
as swiftly as you have opened it
i didn't mean to
i just wanted to feel comfortable
instead of feeling hurt being around you

broken

i have broken us
your distance reminds me of this

lost again

it feels like i have lost you again
first time was finding out you're engaged
this time is finding out you're getting married

not happening

"it's all happening for us" you said with a smile
echoed inside my head in response
"no, my love. it's not happening for me the way i wanted
i watch you fall deeper in love with someone else everyday
when what i wanted is to make you mine."

this is how i feel

i don't know how you feel about me
but i know how i feel about you
i can stare at you all day
it makes me happy and bring smiles to my face

i don't need to talk and i'm happily just listening to you
or we both don't have to talk and just listen to tunes
i just love the way you look and
i'm happy just holding you in my arms and kiss you repeatedly

that's how i feel about you
that's love, i think
and that's what i feel when i'm with you

again

the news of you getting married opened up my wound
i feel as though i have lost you the second time
the difference is this time i'm not strong enough
to hide my broken heart in front of you
fight or flight
i chose latter, again

tuesday

i played our mix tape the other day
and you're going to get married in two days
i want to be happy for you
but my heart wants what it wants

i'm afraid to see you again
i know i have to face you when tuesday comes
my heart races just thinking about it
it's protecting me from you
you, what it wants and yet it protects itself from you

it's confusing, just like how you feel about me
i know deep down you feel something for me
i hope that one day we could talk about it so that i can truly move on
i'm wishing that one day would be tuesday to come
coz i really want to know how you feel about me

hide & seek

your eyes searched for mine
i looked anywhere but your way
for every time i look at you
i want to throw myself into your arms
feel your heartbeat against my cheek
taking what wasn't mine

our eyes play hide and seek
you walked violently through the air before me
i felt the gust of your discomfort
my heart slammed its pulses against my chest
until i finally smiled and looked you in the eyes
oh, how much i really wanted you to know the truth
i love you more than meets the eye

embrace

because of you
i embrace my vulnerabilities

poems for you

poems i have written for you
not just for your birthday
i hope to give them to you someday

i ought to

i wanted to know why you held onto my hand tightly
i ought to stay and ask you not to let me go
in that moment i truly thought you have fallen
it won't matter now that you are married
you looked happy in your wedding photos
i ought to move on and let you go

cut cut cut

i could cut someone off without feeling guilty
i don't understand why i hold onto you for so long and so dearly
i want to disconnect for a reason i can't disclose
i'm sure you could figure it out if i let you come close

the "un-scary" scary thirty

you have said "check in with the 89ers
turning 30 this year"
here's a box of goodies
helping you through this "un-scary" scary year

thirty isn't scary
speaking from memory
you become a wiser learner
and an unwilling teacher
sweet, savoury, healthy and naughty
like this treasure box
full of variety

food is happiness
full of memories
thirty isn't all that scary
you will learn to embrace this journey

the last gift

i wanted to give you something to remember me by
what would be better than a poem that was left nearby
a gift that comforts and brings love to your heart
i don’t think you realise this would be the last gift you will find

heartache

i feel an ache from a distance
i focus on pinpointing its origin
i notice it gets stronger
i sense it travels in my arm
and wondering why it's in my left arm

the ache gets more intense
until it hits the center of my palm
it stops and remains for a few seconds
then i feel another ache from a distance
this cycle repeats itself until i stop thinking
until i stop thinking of the person who broke my heart
that's what heartbreak feels like

an ache travels from my heart into my left palm
attempting to escape my body
so that my heart can start healing

a gift to myself

i showered you with gifts
hoping to make you fall in love with me
i actually gave myself the rarest gift
a realisation that you actually don't give a fuck about me

regret

i regret showing you the caring and loving i shouldn't have
you treat me like a distant stranger to exchange daily pleasantries with
you expect to be showered with love so you feel adored and admired
i haven't been and never will be on your mind
while you're an image of regret seared into my mind

thoughtfulness

you wouldn't care if i stopped being thoughtful
i'm not just a thoughtful human being
you just hadn't noticed how special you are to me

lost & found

what’s mine will find me
you are lost
i found me

lost count

i have lost count of the times you're forgiven by me
i have lost count of the times you ignored me
i have lost count of the times my anxiety strikes me
i have lost count of the times you unexpectedly touched me

i have lost count of the times i think about you
i have lost count of the times i smiled when i'm reminded of you
i have lost count of the times i picked myself up when i can't have you
i haven't lost count of the times i stopped myself from wanting you
it's all the time

****my addiction to you****

i don't know why i'm so drawn towards you
i have tried drowning you out with a busy life
i find myself being pulled back towards you
i can only accept this is how i feel about you
i know the feeling isn't mutual
but that doesn't stop me from feeling it

i wanted to see how happy you are in your married life
like i'm addicted to the pain from a heartbreak
i injected myself with this pain at the thought of you
so that i can move on quickly

when i see you the next day
you mended the cracks in my heart with your smiles
my heart struggles to beat in a steady rhythm
as though it's trying to break free from this mend
just so it could feel pain again
i still have love for you but you love someone else

your words

your eyes speak one truth
contradicts your words
consistency is what i want from you

i can't look at you without wondering
what is the truth?

breathing heavily to calm my thoughts
you take it all away with a smile
can i trust that too?

final bye

i gave you my final gift
a tenderness that i could ever give
meeting you was my gift
you've shown me how i should live

hello

everytime you said hello
i picked up my pen
all the poems i have
confirmed how i feel about you

breathe

when i long for your touch
i pick up london brit and breathe
breathe
breathe
breathe
breathe
breathe

amazing grace

i mesmerised why i couldn't have you
"this is amazing grace" comes on the radio

see

before i learn to see
skin deep is all i could see
now that i have learned to truly see
i see more than my eyes could see

twin flames

i couldn't wish for a better person to show me
what i have been missing and why i need to lean on somebody

i didn't know why your warmth makes me fall deeply
until twin flames was explained to me

after twin flames meeting comes the running and chasing
i wonder if you realised you're going through this stage of growing

you once denied to be an emotional Cancer
your recent post told me that you have begun to embrace your true nature

until you awaken your soul like i have
the push-pull will continue to dominate our union

belonged

when you don't belong
you always long
the more you long
you'll end up on your own

unreciprocated is a poetry collection about
love, heartache, rejection, acceptance, hope and healing
the poems are arranged in the order that the poems were written

unreciprocated takes readers through the writer's journey of
finding love, enduring pain from heartbreak,
overcoming rejection and discovering hope through healing

www.ingramcontent.com/pod-product-compliance
Lightning Source LLC
Chambersburg PA
CBHW020559030426
42337CB00013B/1146
* 9 7 8 0 6 4 6 8 1 3 8 1 3 *